★ THE ★
UNITED
STATES
PRESIDENTS

WARREN G. HARDING

Heidi M.D. Elston

**Checkerboard
Library**

An Imprint of Abdo Publishing
abdobooks.com

ABDOBOOKS.COM

Published by Abdo Publishing, a division of ABDO, PO Box 398166, Minneapolis, Minnesota 55439. Copyright © 2021 by Abdo Consulting Group, Inc. International copyrights reserved in all countries. No part of this book may be reproduced in any form without written permission from the publisher. Checkerboard Library™ is a trademark and logo of Abdo Publishing.

Printed in the United States of America, North Mankato, Minnesota
052020
092020

Design: Emily O'Malley, Kelly Doudna, Mighty Media, Inc.
Production: Mighty Media, Inc.
Editor: Jessica Rusick

Cover Photograph: Getty Images
Interior Photographs: Albert de Bruijn/iStockphoto, p. 37; AP Images, pp. 21, 36; David J. Frent/Getty Images, p. 24; Getty Images, pp. 5, 12; Hulton Archive/Getty Images, p. 31; Library of Congress, pp. 6 (Florence Harding), 7, 19, 20, 22, 27, 29, 40; MPI/Getty Images, p. 15; National Archives and Records Administration, pp. 7 (Nineteenth Amendment), 23 (Nineteenth Amendment); National Baseball Hall of Fame Library/Getty Images, p. 13; Ohio Historical Society, pp. 14, 17, 23, 33; Paul Popper/Popperfoto/Getty Images, p. 32; Pete Souza/Flickr, p. 44; Shutterstock Images, pp. 6 (Harding's birthplace), 11, 38, 39; Topical Press Agency/Getty Images, p. 25; Wikimedia Commons, pp. 6, 40 (Washington), 42

Library of Congress Control Number: 2019956484

Publisher's Cataloging-in-Publication Data
Names: Elston, Heidi M.D., author.
Title: Warren G. Harding / by Heidi M.D. Elston
Description: Minneapolis, Minnesota : Abdo Publishing, 2021 | Series: The United States presidents | Includes online resources and index.
Identifiers: ISBN 9781532193521 (lib. bdg.) | ISBN 9781098212162 (ebook)
Subjects: LCSH: Harding, Warren G. (Warren Gamaliel), 1865-1923--Juvenile literature. | Presidents—Biography--Juvenile literature. | Presidents--United States--History--Juvenile literature. | Legislators—United States--Biography--Juvenile literature. | Politics and government--Biography--Juvenile literature.
Classification: DDC 973.914092--dc23

★ CONTENTS ★

Warren G. Harding

Warren G. Harding was the twenty-ninth president of the United States. He won the 1920 election by more than 7 million **popular votes**.

As a young man, Harding bought a struggling newspaper and made it a success. He later became a US senator. As a senator, Harding did his best to help Americans. Yet, he wanted to reach more people. So, in 1920, Harding ran for president of the United States.

World War I had recently ended. Many Americans were out of work and had little money. Harding promised to return the country to a simpler, easier time. He easily won the election.

President Harding was popular. But his **administration** suffered through **scandals**. Still, Harding remained honest and worked hard for the people.

After less than three years as president, Harding died. He was the sixth US president to die in office. After Harding's death, **Republican** presidents continued to follow his policies through the 1920s.

TIMELINE

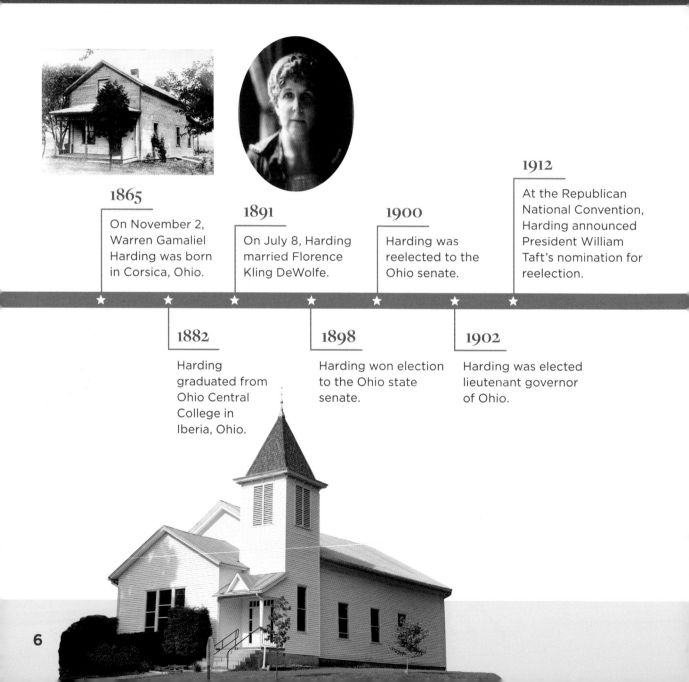

1865

On November 2, Warren Gamaliel Harding was born in Corsica, Ohio.

1882

Harding graduated from Ohio Central College in Iberia, Ohio.

1891

On July 8, Harding married Florence Kling DeWolfe.

1898

Harding won election to the Ohio state senate.

1900

Harding was reelected to the Ohio senate.

1902

Harding was elected lieutenant governor of Ohio.

1912

At the Republican National Convention, Harding announced President William Taft's nomination for reelection.

1919

The Eighteenth Amendment was approved on January 29. It banned the manufacture and sale of alcohol. In October, Congress adopted the Volstead Act to enforce the amendment.

1921

Harding was inaugurated as the twenty-ninth US president on March 4.

1923

Harding went on a speaking tour across the nation. On August 2, President Warren G. Harding died.

1917

The United States entered World War I.

1914

Harding won election to the US Senate.

1918

The Allies won World War I.

1920

On August 26, the Nineteenth Amendment was added to the US Constitution. This gave all women the right to vote. Harding campaigned for president with the slogan "Back to Normalcy." On November 2, Harding won the election.

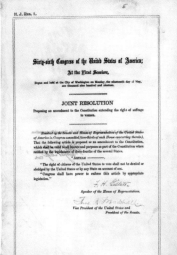

" We must have a citizenship less concerned about what the government can do for it and more anxious about **what it can do for the nation."**

WARREN G. HARDING

DID YOU KNOW?

★ Warren G. Harding was the first president to ride in an automobile to and from his inauguration.

★ Harding was the first president to have a radio in the White House. And, he was the first president to give a speech over the radio.

★ President Harding dedicated the Lincoln Memorial on May 30, 1922. The Lincoln Memorial honors the sixteenth US president, Abraham Lincoln. It is located in Washington, DC.

★ Harding wore size 14 shoes! Of all US presidents, Harding's feet were the largest.

★ Harding's dog Laddie Boy had a birthday party at the White House. A frosted cake made from dog biscuits was served.

Growing Up in Ohio

Warren Gamaliel Harding was born on November 2, 1865, in Corsica, Ohio. Corsica is now called Blooming Grove. Warren's parents were George Tryon and Phoebe Dickerson Harding.

George supported his family by farming. He was also a country doctor and a trader. Phoebe was a **midwife**. Still, the Harding family was poor.

Warren was the first of eight children. Growing up, he spent much of his time doing chores. These included cutting down trees, chopping wood, and planting and harvesting crops.

Eventually, Warren's father became part owner of a weekly newspaper. It was called the *Caledonia Argus*. Warren helped any way he could. He soon learned to set **type**. Warren discovered he liked the newspaper business.

★ ✶
✶

FAST FACTS

BORN: November 2, 1865

WIFE: Florence Kling DeWolfe (1860–1924)

CHILDREN: none

POLITICAL PARTY: Republican

AGE AT INAUGURATION: 55

YEARS SERVED: 1921–1923

VICE PRESIDENT: Calvin Coolidge

DIED: August 2, 1923, age 57

Warren's birthplace

Warren attended a one-room school in Caledonia, Ohio. When he was 14, he entered Ohio Central College in Iberia, Ohio. There, Warren was popular. He edited the yearbook and entered speaking contests. Also, he played the alto horn. Warren graduated in 1882.

First Jobs

After graduation, Harding moved to Marion, Ohio. His family had moved there while he was in school. In Marion, Harding managed the Marion Citizens' Cornet Band. He also played sports, such as baseball.

During this time, Harding held many jobs. He taught school for one term. Harding also studied law. Then, he worked as a salesman.

Harding did not like any of these jobs. He remembered how much he had enjoyed the newspaper business. When he was 19, Harding became a reporter for the *Mirror*. The *Mirror* was a **Democratic** weekly newspaper in Marion. However, Harding was already establishing himself as a loyal **Republican**.

Harding later said teaching was "the hardest job I ever had."

Harding (*left*) remained a fan of baseball. While president, he entertained professional baseball player Babe Ruth (*right*) at the White House.

During the 1884 presidential campaign, Harding supported **Republican** candidate James G. Blaine. He even wore a Blaine campaign hat to work. This upset the newspaper owners, so they fired Harding.

The *Marion Star*

In just a few weeks, Harding moved on to a different newspaper. The *Marion Star* was for sale for $300. Harding and two friends bought it. Now, Harding was a newspaper publisher!

Most people believed Harding was foolish to buy the *Marion Star*. Its equipment badly needed repair.

Harding working at the *Marion Star*. He is the first newspaper publisher to become a US president.

The newspaper did not have enough advertising money coming in. And, each **subscription** brought in only ten cents a week.

To help the newspaper succeed, Harding worked day and night. He operated the equipment, wrote articles, and sold advertising space.

Harding got help after he met Florence Kling DeWolfe. Florence had been born in Marion in 1860. The two fell in love and married on July 8, 1891. They had no children together.

Mrs. Harding began working at the *Marion Star.* Harding trusted his wife's

Harding nicknamed his wife "The Duchess."

good business sense. Slowly, she took over managing the newspaper. Mrs. Harding's hard work made it a success.

Entering Politics

Now, Harding had more time for other interests. He wanted to make his community and state a better place to live. So, Harding entered politics. He went to town meetings and gave speeches. People liked his ideas. Harding soon made a name for himself as a skillful speaker.

Harding was elected to the Ohio state senate in 1898. There, he became one of the most popular senators. Harding was friendly. And, he helped keep peace within the **Republican** Party. Harding was reelected in 1900. He then became a party leader.

In 1902, Harding was elected lieutenant governor of Ohio. Harding ran for governor of Ohio in 1910. He lost the election. Harding's political career seemed over.

Then in 1912, Harding gave an important speech at the **Republican National Convention**. There, he announced President William Taft's nomination for reelection. Harding impressed Republican Party leaders with his speaking ability.

The Hardings built their Marion, Ohio, home in 1891. Harding conducted his 1920 presidential campaign from this home's large porch.

Senator Harding

In 1914, Harding ran for the US Senate. He easily won the election. As a senator, Harding never introduced any major bills. But he was well-liked and popular.

During this time, many countries were fighting **World War I.** President Woodrow Wilson called a special meeting of Congress on April 2, 1917. He wanted the United States to enter the war and help the **Allies** win.

Eighty-two senators voted to go to war. Just six senators voted no. So, the United States went to war. In November 1918, the Allies won. On June 28, 1919, the Treaty of Versailles was signed in France. This officially declared peace between Germany and the Allies.

Following the war, President Wilson asked Congress to officially approve the Treaty of Versailles. But Harding and many other **Republicans** strongly opposed him. They did not like the **League of Nations** agreement included in the treaty. The Senate defeated the treaty on November 19, 1919. The United States made a separate peace agreement with Germany in 1921.

Harding served in the US Senate for six years.

Prohibition

As a senator, Harding voted for two **amendments** to the US **Constitution**. The Eighteenth Amendment stopped the manufacture and sale of alcohol in America. This was also known as the Prohibition Amendment. It was officially approved on January 29, 1919.

US officials destroying alcohol

In October, Congress adopted the Volstead Act. This act provided for the enforcement of the Eighteenth Amendment. Still, enforcement varied. It was weaker in cities than in rural areas. This is because people in large cities strongly opposed Prohibition.

Prohibition ended the legal sale of alcohol in the United States. But people did not stop drinking it. Illegal sales of alcohol rose. And a new

Al Capone made about $60 million
a year bootlegging.

kind of criminal emerged. Bootleggers illegally supplied
alcohol. Al Capone is one of the most famous bootleggers
in US history.

Women's Right to Vote

Senator Harding also voted for the Nineteenth **Amendment**. It gave women in all states the right to vote. The Nineteenth Amendment became part of the US **Constitution** on August 26, 1920.

Women had been fighting for the right to vote since the early 1800s.

Similar amendments had been introduced in Congress in 1878 and 1914. But both proposals had been defeated.

Wyoming had been the first state to allow women the right to vote. It had become a state in 1890 with a constitution allowing for this privilege. By 1918, women had equal voting rights with men in 15 states.

People kept fighting for equal women's voting rights throughout the country. The Nineteenth Amendment was an important victory.

H. J. Res. 1.

5

Sixty-sixth Congress of the United States of America;

At the First Session,

Begun and held at the City of Washington on Monday, the nineteenth day of May, one thousand nine hundred and nineteen.

JOINT RESOLUTION

Proposing an amendment to the Constitution extending the right of suffrage to women.

Resolved by the Senate and House of Representatives of the United States of America in Congress assembled (two-thirds of each House concurring therein), That the following article is proposed as an amendment to the Constitution, which shall be valid to all intents and purposes as part of the Constitution when ratified by the legislatures of three-fourths of the several States.

"Article ———

"The right of citizens of the United States to vote shall not be denied or abridged by the United States or by any State on account of sex.

"Congress shall have power to enforce this article by appropriate legislation."

F. H. Gillett

Speaker of the House of Representatives.

Thos. R. Marshall

Vice President of the United States and President of the Senate.

Because of the Nineteenth Amendment (*right*), Mrs. Harding (*above*) was the first First Lady able to vote for her husband.

The 1920 Election

In 1920, Harding wanted to run for senator again. But that year, the **Republican** Party couldn't agree on a choice for president. Some Republican leaders began mentioning Harding as a possible candidate.

UNDER
The 19th
Amendment
I CAST MY
FIRST VOTE
Nov. 2nd, 1920

Harding
Coolidge

The Straight
Republican
Ticket

Lancaster, Pa.

A campaign ribbon from the 1920 election

Later that year, Republican delegates nominated Harding for president. They chose Massachusetts governor Calvin Coolidge as his **running mate**. The **Democrats** chose Ohio governor James M. Cox to run for president. Franklin D. Roosevelt was nominated for vice president.

At this time, the US **economy** was suffering. Businesses were failing, and people were losing their jobs. Americans blamed President Wilson and his fellow Democrats.

Harding promised to make the country better. He campaigned on the **slogan** "Back to Normalcy."

Calvin Coolidge (*left*) with Harding

On November 2, Harding won the election! He received more than 16 million **popular votes**. Cox won fewer than 10 million. Harding was the first president for whom all women could vote.

President Harding

On March 4, 1921, Harding was **inaugurated** as the **twenty-ninth US president.** He wanted to return the country to normalcy. So, Harding got right to work on keeping this campaign promise.

To help the US **economy**, President Harding supported new laws. He allowed US businesses to produce more goods. He also lowered taxes on goods made in America. But Harding raised taxes on products from other countries. The Fordney-McCumber Act of 1922 raised **tariffs** to the highest in history! The act was meant to help farmers and other American workers.

Harding also had success in foreign affairs. He called for the Washington Conference. There, leaders arranged treaties that limited the naval strengths of world powers.

President Harding also took a stand on labor. At the time, the nation's large steel companies had 12-hour workdays. Harding convinced the steel companies to shorten the workday.

President Harding's inauguration

PRESIDENT HARDING'S CABINET

ONE TERM

March 4, 1921–August 2, 1923

- ★ **STATE:** Charles Evans Hughes
- ★ **TREASURY:** Andrew W. Mellon
- ★ **WAR:** John Wingate Weeks
- ★ **NAVY:** Edwin Denby
- ★ **ATTORNEY GENERAL:** Harry Micajah Daugherty
- ★ **INTERIOR:** Albert Bacon Fall
  Hubert Work (from March 5, 1923)
- ★ **AGRICULTURE:** Henry Cantwell Wallace
- ★ **COMMERCE:** Herbert Hoover
- ★ **LABOR:** James John Davis

President Harding (*seated, third from right*), Vice President Coolidge (*seated, second from right*), and cabinet members

Teapot Dome Scandal

President Harding was working hard. The American people had faith in him. But there were problems within his **administration**. Congress uncovered crimes in the Justice Department and the Veterans Bureau. And some members of Harding's **cabinet** were dishonest.

Albert B. Fall was President Harding's secretary of the interior. He was in charge of America's natural resources. Fall led the Harding administration into one of the greatest **scandals** in US history. It is called the Teapot Dome scandal.

Teapot Dome was a piece of government land in Wyoming. Fall secretly allowed only Harry F. Sinclair of the Mammoth Oil Company to drill on this land. In return, Fall received bribes. Fall later went to jail for his part in the scandal.

President Harding was not charged with any wrongdoing for Fall's actions. However, the scandal took a toll on Harding's health.

SUPREME COURT APPOINTMENTS

WILLIAM TAFT: 1921

GEORGE SUTHERLAND: 1922

PIERCE BUTLER: 1923

EDWARD T. SANFORD: 1923

Albert B. Fall (*left*) with Harry F. Sinclair

Speaking Tour

Meanwhile, the **Republicans** had lost many seats in Congress during the 1922 elections. President Harding was deeply upset. He wanted to rebuild trust in his **administration**. So, in 1923, he decided to take a speaking tour to talk to Americans. The trip would take him across the country, including Alaska.

President and Mrs. Harding traveled together across the country. Harding was the first president to visit Alaska and Canada while in office.

While in Seattle, Washington, President Harding fell ill. He then traveled to California. In San Francisco on August 2, 1923, President Warren G. Harding died. Then, Vice President Coolidge became president.

Harding was buried in Marion. Florence Harding died in Marion the next year. She was buried next to her husband.

Warren G. Harding was a popular president. Sadly, his presidency is remembered for the

In Marion, a group of citizens raised money for Harding's tomb.

scandals that tarnished his **cabinet**. Harding desired to be America's "best-loved" president. He wanted to restore the war-weary country to a time of normalcy. Harding worked hard to achieve this goal and be a good leader.

BRANCHES OF GOVERNMENT

The US government is divided into three branches. They are the executive, legislative, and judicial branches. This division is called a separation of powers. Each branch has some power over the others. This is called a system of checks and balances.

★ EXECUTIVE BRANCH

The executive branch enforces laws. It is made up of the president, the vice president, and the president's cabinet. The president represents the United States around the world. He or she oversees relations with other countries and signs treaties. The president signs bills into law and appoints officials and federal judges. He or she also leads the military and manages government workers.

★ LEGISLATIVE BRANCH

The legislative branch makes laws, maintains the military, and regulates trade. It also has the power to declare war. This branch consists of the Senate and the House of Representatives. Together, these two houses make up Congress. Each state has two senators. A state's population determines the number of representatives it has.

★ JUDICIAL BRANCH

The judicial branch interprets laws. It consists of district courts, courts of appeals, and the Supreme Court. District courts try cases. If a person disagrees with a trial's outcome, he or she may appeal. If a court of appeals supports the ruling, a person may appeal to the Supreme Court. The Supreme Court also makes sure that laws follow the US Constitution.

THE PRESIDENT ★

★ QUALIFICATIONS FOR OFFICE

To be president, a person must meet three requirements. A candidate must be at least 35 years old and a natural-born US citizen. He or she must also have lived in the United States for at least 14 years.

★ ELECTORAL COLLEGE

The US presidential election is an indirect election. Voters from each state choose electors to represent them in the Electoral College. The number of electors from each state is based on the state's population. Each elector has one electoral vote. Electors are pledged to cast their vote for the candidate who receives the highest number of popular votes in their state. A candidate must receive the majority of Electoral College votes to win.

★ TERM OF OFFICE

Each president may be elected to two four-year terms. Sometimes, a president may only be elected once. This happens if he or she served more than two years of the previous president's term.

The presidential election is held on the Tuesday after the first Monday in November. The president is sworn in on January 20 of the following year. At that time, he or she takes the oath of office:

> *I do solemnly swear (or affirm) that I will faithfully execute the office of President of the United States, and will to the best of my ability, preserve, protect and defend the Constitution of the United States.*

LINE OF SUCCESSION

The Presidential Succession Act of 1947 defines who becomes president if the president cannot serve. The vice president is first in the line of succession. Next are the Speaker of the House and the President Pro Tempore of the Senate. If none of these individuals is able to serve, the office falls to the president's cabinet members. They would take office in the order in which each department was created:

Secretary of State

Secretary of the Treasury

Secretary of Defense

Attorney General

Secretary of the Interior

Secretary of Agriculture

Secretary of Commerce

Secretary of Labor

Secretary of Health and Human Services

Secretary of Housing and Urban Development

Secretary of Transportation

Secretary of Energy

Secretary of Education

Secretary of Veterans Affairs

Secretary of Homeland Security

While in office, the president receives a salary of $400,000 each year. He or she lives in the White House and has 24-hour Secret Service protection.

The president may travel on a Boeing 747 jet called Air Force One. The airplane can accommodate 76 passengers. It has kitchens, a dining room, sleeping areas, and a conference room. It also has fully equipped offices with the latest communications systems. Air Force One can fly halfway around the world before needing to refuel. It can even refuel in flight!

Air Force One

If the president wishes to travel by car, he or she uses Cadillac One. It has been modified with heavy armor and communications systems. The president takes

Cadillac One

Cadillac One along when visiting other countries if secure transportation will be needed.

The president also travels on a helicopter called Marine One. Like the presidential car, Marine One accompanies the president when traveling abroad if necessary.

Sometimes, the president needs to get away and relax with family and friends. Camp David is the official presidential retreat. It is located in the cool, wooded mountains of Maryland. The US Navy maintains the retreat, and the US Marine Corps keeps it secure. The camp offers swimming, tennis, golf, and hiking.

When the president leaves office, he or she receives lifetime Secret Service protection. He or she also receives a yearly pension of $207,800 and funding for office space, supplies, and staff.

Marine One

George Washington

Abraham Lincoln

Theodore Roosevelt

	PRESIDENT	PARTY	TOOK OFFICE
1	George Washington	None	April 30, 1789
2	John Adams	Federalist	March 4, 1797
3	Thomas Jefferson	Democratic-Republican	March 4, 1801
4	James Madison	Democratic-Republican	March 4, 1809
5	James Monroe	Democratic-Republican	March 4, 1817
6	John Quincy Adams	Democratic-Republican	March 4, 1825
7	Andrew Jackson	Democrat	March 4, 1829
8	Martin Van Buren	Democrat	March 4, 1837
9	William H. Harrison	Whig	March 4, 1841
10	John Tyler	Whig	April 6, 1841
11	James K. Polk	Democrat	March 4, 1845
12	Zachary Taylor	Whig	March 5, 1849
13	Millard Fillmore	Whig	July 10, 1850
14	Franklin Pierce	Democrat	March 4, 1853
15	James Buchanan	Democrat	March 4, 1857
16	Abraham Lincoln	Republican	March 4, 1861
17	Andrew Johnson	Democrat	April 15, 1865
18	Ulysses S. Grant	Republican	March 4, 1869
19	Rutherford B. Hayes	Republican	March 3, 1877

THEIR TERMS ⭐

LEFT OFFICE	TERMS SERVED	VICE PRESIDENT
March 4, 1797	Two	John Adams
March 4, 1801	One	Thomas Jefferson
March 4, 1809	Two	Aaron Burr, George Clinton
March 4, 1817	Two	George Clinton, Elbridge Gerry
March 4, 1825	Two	Daniel D. Tompkins
March 4, 1829	One	John C. Calhoun
March 4, 1837	Two	John C. Calhoun, Martin Van Buren
March 4, 1841	One	Richard M. Johnson
April 4, 1841	Died During First Term	John Tyler
March 4, 1845	Completed Harrison's Term	Office Vacant
March 4, 1849	One	George M. Dallas
July 9, 1850	Died During First Term	Millard Fillmore
March 4, 1853	Completed Taylor's Term	Office Vacant
March 4, 1857	One	William R.D. King
March 4, 1861	One	John C. Breckinridge
April 15, 1865	Served One Term, Died During Second Term	Hannibal Hamlin, Andrew Johnson
March 4, 1869	Completed Lincoln's Second Term	Office Vacant
March 4, 1877	Two	Schuyler Colfax, Henry Wilson
March 4, 1881	One	William A. Wheeler

Franklin D. Roosevelt

John F. Kennedy

Ronald Reagan

	PRESIDENT	PARTY	TOOK OFFICE
20	James A. Garfield	Republican	March 4, 1881
21	Chester Arthur	Republican	September 20, 1881
22	Grover Cleveland	Democrat	March 4, 1885
23	Benjamin Harrison	Republican	March 4, 1889
24	Grover Cleveland	Democrat	March 4, 1893
25	William McKinley	Republican	March 4, 1897
26	Theodore Roosevelt	Republican	September 14, 1901
27	William Taft	Republican	March 4, 1909
28	Woodrow Wilson	Democrat	March 4, 1913
29	Warren G. Harding	Republican	March 4, 1921
30	Calvin Coolidge	Republican	August 3, 1923
31	Herbert Hoover	Republican	March 4, 1929
32	Franklin D. Roosevelt	Democrat	March 4, 1933
33	Harry S. Truman	Democrat	April 12, 1945
34	Dwight D. Eisenhower	Republican	January 20, 1953
35	John F. Kennedy	Democrat	January 20, 1961

LEFT OFFICE	TERMS SERVED	VICE PRESIDENT
September 19, 1881	Died During First Term	Chester Arthur
March 4, 1885	Completed Garfield's Term	Office Vacant
March 4, 1889	One	Thomas A. Hendricks
March 4, 1893	One	Levi P. Morton
March 4, 1897	One	Adlai E. Stevenson
September 14, 1901	Served One Term, Died During Second Term	Garret A. Hobart, Theodore Roosevelt
March 4, 1909	Completed McKinley's Second Term, Served One Term	Office Vacant, Charles Fairbanks
March 4, 1913	One	James S. Sherman
March 4, 1921	Two	Thomas R. Marshall
August 2, 1923	Died During First Term	Calvin Coolidge
March 4, 1929	Completed Harding's Term, Served One Term	Office Vacant, Charles Dawes
March 4, 1933	One	Charles Curtis
April 12, 1945	Served Three Terms, Died During Fourth Term	John Nance Garner, Henry A. Wallace, Harry S. Truman
January 20, 1953	Completed Roosevelt's Fourth Term, Served One Term	Office Vacant, Alben Barkley
January 20, 1961	Two	Richard Nixon
November 22, 1963	Died During First Term	Lyndon B. Johnson

	PRESIDENT	PARTY	TOOK OFFICE
36	Lyndon B. Johnson	Democrat	November 22, 1963
37	Richard Nixon	Republican	January 20, 1969
38	Gerald Ford	Republican	August 9, 1974
39	Jimmy Carter	Democrat	January 20, 1977
40	Ronald Reagan	Republican	January 20, 1981
41	George H.W. Bush	Republican	January 20, 1989
42	Bill Clinton	Democrat	January 20, 1993
43	George W. Bush	Republican	January 20, 2001
44	Barack Obama	Democrat	January 20, 2009
45	Donald Trump	Republican	January 20, 2017

Barack Obama

★ PRESIDENTS MATH GAME ★

Have fun with this presidents math game! First, study the list above
and memorize each president's name and number. Then, use math
to figure out which president completes each equation below.

1. Warren G. Harding − Franklin Pierce = ?

2. Thomas Jefferson + Warren G. Harding = ?

3. Warren G. Harding − Andrew Jackson = ?

3. Grover Cleveland (29 − 7 = 22)
2. Franklin D. Roosevelt (3 + 29 = 32)
Answers: 1. James Buchanan (29 − 14 = 15)

LEFT OFFICE	TERMS SERVED	VICE PRESIDENT
January 20, 1969	Completed Kennedy's Term, Served One Term	Office Vacant, Hubert H. Humphrey
August 9, 1974	Completed First Term, Resigned During Second Term	Spiro T. Agnew, Gerald Ford
January 20, 1977	Completed Nixon's Second Term	Nelson A. Rockefeller
January 20, 1981	One	Walter Mondale
January 20, 1989	Two	George H.W. Bush
January 20, 1993	One	Dan Quayle
January 20, 2001	Two	Al Gore
January 20, 2009	Two	Dick Cheney
January 20, 2017	Two	Joe Biden
		Mike Pence

WRITE TO THE PRESIDENT

You may write to the president at:

The White House
1600 Pennsylvania Avenue NW
Washington, DC 20500

You may email the president at:

www.whitehouse.gov/contact

★ GLOSSARY ★

administration—the people who manage a presidential government.

allies—people, groups, or nations united for some special purpose. During World War I, Great Britain, France, Russia, Italy, and Japan were called the Allies.

amendment—a change to a country's constitution.

cabinet—a group of advisers chosen by the president to lead government departments.

constitution—the laws that govern a country or a state. The US Constitution is the laws that govern the United States.

Democrat—a member of the Democratic political party. Democrats believe in social change and strong government.

economy—the way a nation uses its money, goods, and natural resources.

inaugurate (ih-NAW-gyuh-rayt)—to swear into a political office.

League of Nations—an international association created to maintain peace among the nations of the world.

midwife—a person who assists women in childbirth.

popular vote—the vote of the entire body of people with the right to vote.

Republican—a member of the Republican political party. Republicans are conservative and believe in small government.

Republican National Convention—a national meeting held every four years during which the Republican Party chooses its candidates for president and vice president.

running mate—a candidate running for a lower-rank position on an election ticket, especially the candidate for vice president.

scandal—an action that shocks people and disgraces those connected with it.

slogan—a word or a phrase used to express a position, a stand, or a goal.

subscription—a purchase by prepayment for a certain number of issues of a publication, such as a newspaper or a magazine.

tariff—the taxes a government puts on imported or exported goods.

type—a piece of metal or wood bearing on the upper surface a raised letter, number, or other figure for use in printing.

World War I—from 1914 to 1918, fought in Europe. Great Britain, France, Russia, the United States, and their allies were on one side. Germany, Austria-Hungary, and their allies were on the other side.

ONLINE RESOURCES

Booklinks
NONFICTION NETWORK
FREE! ONLINE NONFICTION RESOURCES

To learn more about Warren G. Harding, please visit **abdobooklinks.com** or scan this QR code. These links are routinely monitored and updated to provide the most current information available.

★ INDEX ★